LYNNE NANNEN ROBERTSON, Ph.D., R.D., L.D.

Productivity in Foodservice

IOWA STATE UNIVERSITY PRESS / AMES

Lynne Nannen Robertson, Ph.D., R.D., L.D., is president of Creative Concepts, a foodservice consulting firm. Dr. Robertson teaches all phases of foodservice management to dietitians and managers throughout the United States.

© 1991 Iowa State University Press, Ames, Iowa 50014

♾ Printed on acid-free paper in the United States of America

Originally published in 1972 as *Work Simplification in Food Service: Individualized Instruction* through nine printings (1972–1990)
This edition, 1991
    Second printing, 1993
    Third printing, 1994
    Fourth printing, 1996

Library of Congress Cataloging-in-Publication Data

Robertson, Lynne Nannen
    Productivity in foodservice / Lynne Nannen Robertson.
        p.   cm.
    Rev. ed. of: Work simplification in food service / Lynne Nannen Ross. 1972.
    ISBN 0-8138-0784-0 (alk. paper)
    1. Food service.   2. Methods engineering.   I. Ross, Lynne Nannen.
    Work simplification in food service.   II. Title.
    TX943.R68   1991
    647.95 — dc20   90–46631

Contents

Preface

In this time of rising costs, administrators and foodservice directors are looking at every possible way to economize without adversely affecting foodservice quality and the health and welfare of those served. Industrial-engineering techniques can improve productivity in every area and task of foodservice and can contribute to making better use of human and physical resources. This book should help the foodservice employee understand the principles of productivity and their application to food preparation and service. Illustrations reinforce the written material.

The following pages will lead you through the scientific approach to work simplification. Improved productivity is achieved by applying the eight principles of industrial engineering in detail. These principles use time and motion study to make your job easier. The final sections give specific evaluations and applications of the concepts you have studied.

To help you remember, it is suggested that you apply each principle to an activity in your foodservice department before continuing to the next.

COORDINATED ILLUSTRATIVE SLIDES

One hundred colored slides have been coordinated with the key ideas in this manual to further illustrate and clarify the points being studied. The complete set of 100 slides may be ordered from Dr. Lynne N. Robertson, 913 S.E. Chaparal Drive, Ankeny, Iowa 50021, for $80.00.

PRODUCTIVITY IN FOODSERVICE

Your Job Can Be Easier

[1] Work simplification is the process of making a job easier to improve productivity. It is the organized use of common sense to find easier and better ways of doing work. Actually, it is nothing new. The first wheel, the first plow, the first sail are all good examples of age-old uses of modern work simplification methods.

Everyone can benefit by improving productivity, but in the beginning people in supervisory positions will be the ones who must be inspired to lead the way. To achieve the best results, get ideas and suggestions from the personnel working in various jobs.

The human problem to be considered in putting the new method to work is very important. Every time a method is changed, workers are affected. People resist what they do not understand. It is important to explain and demonstrate carefully in an effort to avoid misunderstanding.

The ability to simplify tasks depends upon a frame of mind — a belief that work can be managed and made easier and less time-consuming. People who have this belief are always seeking easier methods of achieving results. Each new task challenges their thinking and their ability to see improvement.

The practice of looking at work with the desire to economize and simplify processes returns an extra dividend to the worker, even beyond the important saving of time and energy. This dividend is a positive and creative attitude.

[2] A major objective is to do better work with greater efficiency. Better work might be expressed by high-quality foodservice, contented guests, cheerful employees, and satisfied management. Greater efficiency can be shown in the savings of time, money, and energy.

3

TIME

Time saved can be seen at both the employee and supervisory level. By using improved work methods, the employee will have time to work at an easy pace, overtime will be eliminated, and accidents reduced. Well-trained employees will require less supervisory attention in arranging for extra help or overtime or even in helping with food production.

MONEY

Money can be saved by reducing the amount of labor needed, the equipment repair caused by misuse, the food wasted through overproduction and unacceptable quality, and caused by carelessness and lack of knowledge.

ENERGY

Energy may be physical, mental, or emotional. The saving of energy can mean the difference between employees who go home exhausted at the end of the day and those who are able to enjoy another eight hours with their families and friends.

Most people confuse speed and hurry, believing the two to be the same. As a matter of fact, when we hurry our work is slowed, unless the hurry is brief. Speed can give good work, because it is obtained by eliminating unnecessary motions. Hurry may result in poor work because it is an acceleration of all the operations, both necessary and unnecessary.

Getting the job done the easiest way is sure to appeal to everyone in the dietary department. Foodservice workers may waste as much time as they spend in actual production. Making workers' time more productive and reducing fatigue is our goal.

IMPROVING PRODUCTIVITY

[3]   **STEP ONE.** The first step in a work simplification program is selecting the job to be improved. The things that need

D.O.T.

improvement are not always apparent. Tackle early those jobs that waste material, energy, and time. A bottleneck job is the best one to investigate. Leave the smooth-flowing jobs alone and attack the holdups. Lengthy jobs offer some of the greatest opportunities for improvement of methods. Chasing around for materials and tools wastes time and energy. Investigate jobs that are repetitious, disliked, monotonous, costly, or difficult as well as jobs that are done frequently.

[4]   **STEP TWO.** The second step toward job improvement requires a detailed breakdown of the job. For successful analysis the individual tasks must be listed detail by detail in the order in which each is performed. This procedure provides an overall picture of the work; flaws can be noticed easily and remedies suggested. All materials handled and all equipment used in doing the work should be included in the breakdown. Be sure to record time spent and distance traveled in performing the task.

Mentally follow a cook through the preparation of an item that is frequently on the menu, for example, macaroni (Fig. 1).

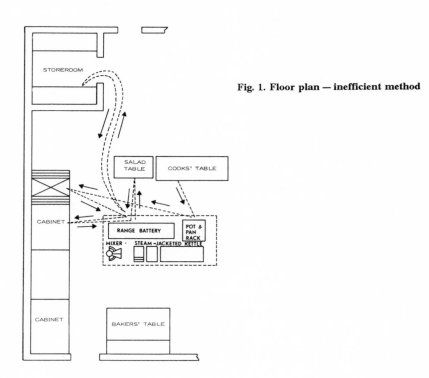

Fig. 1. Floor plan — inefficient method

From the cook's table where the worksheet and recipes are kept, the cook will walk 10 steps to the pot and pan rack to get the pan, 30 steps to the sink to add the desired amount of water. While the water is heating, the cook goes 50 steps to the storeroom for macaroni and returns to the range; 10 steps to the drawer in the salad table for a spoon, then back; 15 steps to a cupboard for salt, then back; and 15 steps again to the sink for a little more water, then back to the range.

[5] **STEP THREE.** The third step toward improved productivity involves asking questions and challenging each operation and detail. It is helpful to ask such questions as:

Why is the job necessary?
Why is it important?
Could the whole job be eliminated?
Can it be changed?
Can parts of the job be combined?
Where should it be done?
Who should do it?
Is each employee doing the job for which he or she is skilled?
When should it be done?
Can self-service be used?
Is there rehandling of food or equipment that could be eliminated?

[6] **STEP FOUR.** The fourth step in implementing a work simplification program is to work out a better method of doing the job. The four procedures that are helpful in improving work methods are (1) eliminate, (2) combine, (3) rearrange, and (4) simplify.

Eliminate the unnecessary steps of the operation. For example, if the coffee cup were served without a saucer, this would eliminate the need to handle the saucer on the serving line and to wash it when the soiled tray is returned.

Combine several steps into one that can be performed more easily and quickly. For example, prepare foods that include dry milk by combining the milk in its dry form with the dry ingredients and the water with the liquid ingredients rather than reconstituting the milk first.

Rearrange materials, equipment, or order of work to make tasks easier to perform. For example, on a tray line, if the work is rearranged so that the soup is served before the crackers it will be easier to be sure that they are not omitted.

Simplify the remaining work that you have determined to be necessary. For example, when serving gelatin salads, the preparation, portioning, and serving of gelatin in a pan will be simpler than using individual molds.

In our example of cooking macaroni, the method worked out in Figure 2 might be a better one. From the baker's table where the worksheet and recipes are kept, proceed 10 steps to the steam-jacketed kettle, turn on the hot water faucet that is located over it, fill the kettle to a predetermined level, and turn on the heat. (While waiting for the water to boil, there are 5 minutes to do another chore.) Just before the water boils, walk 20 steps to the cabinet to get the macaroni and salt, and 20 steps back to the kettle. Add a measured amount of macaroni and salt. Stir with a spoon that is stored on a rack over the kettle.

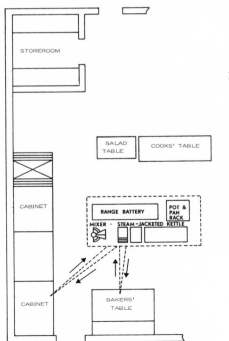

Fig. 2. Floor plan — efficient method

[7]   **STEP FIVE.** The fifth step in a work simplification plan is
applying the new method. After trial and success on a pilot
run, the new method should be put into effect until a better way
is developed.

D.O.T

Before timing an improved method to compare it with the
old one for evaluation, it is important to remember that an
improved method must be practiced several times until it
becomes familiar. An inefficient procedure that has become habit
will seem easier than an efficient new method until it has been
practiced.

To aid in selecting improvement possibilities consider that
each job consists of three parts: (1) *Make Ready,* (2) *Do,* and (3)
Put Away.

Make Ready is the effort and time put into collecting and
setting up the equipment and supplies. An important step in
simplifying a procedure is to combine elements of the Make
Ready step. When setting up trays there are two jobs for which
the work can be made easier by combining operations. Both can
be done during slow periods between meals.

The wrapping of silverware is one example of simplifying a
procedure by combining elements. A knife, fork, and spoon may
be wrapped in a napkin for each person. If soup is served, the
soup spoon should be included also. For liquid diets only the
teaspoon and soup spoon need to be wrapped.

Preparation of a condiment holder is another example of
simplifying a procedure by combining elements. A condiment
holder may be prepared for each person. A name card and/or
menu is attached and the salt, pepper, sugar, salt substitute, etc.,
as prescribed for the diet are included. If desired, catsup,
mustard, etc., may be added. If the unopened preportioned
condiments are kept in a holder with the patient's name on it,
they may be sent back on the tray at the next meal.

One of the most disliked and costly parts of food preparation is the washing of pots and pans. Presoaking can help to
Make Ready the pots and pans so the Do is less difficult. Oil the
sides and bottom of the pan in which the noodles, spaghetti, or
rice are to be cooked to prevent the food from sticking to the
pan.

If noodles or spaghetti are to be cooked in a steam-jacketed kettle, add cooking oil to the boiling water first. This will prevent boiling over. Bring to boil and turn off the heat.

Do is the actual work which is done to provide a service or prepare a product.

Put Away is the cleaning up and storage of equipment and supplies after the product or service is completed. The Put Away step usually involves the process of storing any unused supplies and cleaning the work area. Materials that are used in a particular task should be stored as close as possible to that work area. For example, trays, tray covers, plates, plate covers, and beverage servers used in setting up a tray should be stored so they will be ready for the next meal without additional handling.

The greatest room for improvement lies in the possibility of eliminating the Do operation entirely; for if this is removed, the Make Ready and Put Away that go with it are automatically eliminated also. Make Ready and Put Away add to the cost but not the value of the product of service. For this reason they should be made as efficient as possible.

PRINCIPLE 1 . . .

Make Rhythmic and Smooth-flowing Motions

Smooth, curved motions make use of the momentum of the arm. An overlapping figure-eight stroke (Fig. 3)

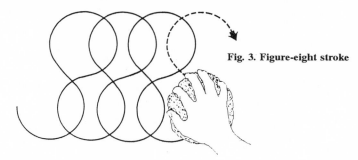

Fig. 3. Figure-eight stroke

and a circular motion (Fig. 4)

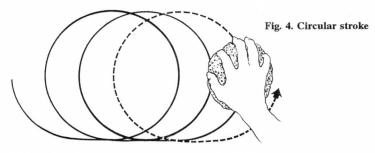

Fig. 4. Circular stroke

11

require less energy than short back and forth strokes (Fig. 5).

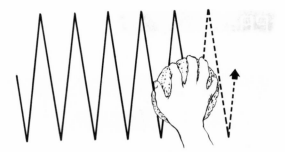

Fig. 5. Back and forth stroke

SCRUBBING

The importance of using the correct stroke can be seen in the simple task of washing off the work area, a task that is done frequently. Floor scrubbing can be done with both improved efficiency and quality by using a figure-eight stroke rather than a back and forth stroke. Mentally mark out an area about 6 feet wide. Start with a soapy mop at one end of the area. Swinging the mop in a figure-eight overlapping stroke back up until reaching the far end. This not only requires less energy and strain on muscles and joints, but also gathers solids into the mop. The soil that is collected can be lifted into the mop bucket. The mop is then rinsed and squeezed almost dry to pick up the cleaning solution that was left on the floor.

SPREADING

[9]   Smooth, continuous, curved motions can be used in spreading batter in a bun or cake pan, frosting a cake or sweet rolls, sharpening a knife, and stirring cereal. To frost a cake efficiently, scoop the frosting in measured amounts to predetermined locations on the cake. The total amount of frosting needed for the cake should be divided into six, eight, or ten equal parts, depending on the size of the cake. These small amounts should

be placed at equal intervals in rows along the ends of the cake. Using a flexible metal spatula, begin at the far side of the cake and spread the frosting in that mound along that side. Gauge the thickness of frosting being spread so that the frosting will last until the first mound at the other end of the cake is reached. Make a figure-eight turn and collect that mound of frosting, spreading it back to the next mound on the original side, again gauging the thickness of frosting being spread so it will completely cover the required area.

SANDWICH MAKING

Another example of a task that should be done with rhythmic, smooth-flowing motions is sandwich making. Place bread in rows on a baking sheet. Four rows of six slices each allow you to make 24 sandwiches at one time. Do this by picking up three slices of bread with each hand and placing them in rows on the baking sheet at the same time. Repeat this procedure four more times to cover the entire tray with 24 slices of bread (Fig. 6).

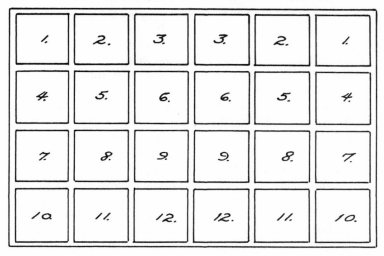

Fig. 6

Without picking up the slices of bread, spread each one to the edges with softened butter or margarine. Place a level scoopful of filling mixture on each slice of bread and spread it evenly to the edges, using one of the strokes illustrated in Figure 7 or another smooth stroke which you may prefer.

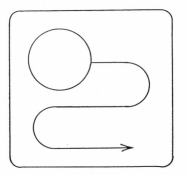 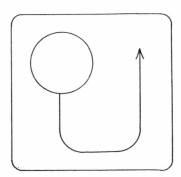

Fig. 7. Spreading filling on bread

Top each slice of bread and filling with two more slices of bread. One of these is the top of the first sandwich and the other is the bottom of the second one. Proceed the same way as for the first layer except six slices in each hand will be required instead of three because two slices will be placed in each location.

Spread butter and filling on each slice of bread. Place a single slice of bread on the top. Each tray will contain 48 complete two-slice sandwiches.

Cover the sandwiches with waxed paper and a damp towel. Refrigerate until serving time. As the sandwiches are served, they may be transferred individually to a cutting board and cut with a sharp knife using the straight downward motion. Either lift the sandwich to the serving plate using a wide, bent spatula or slide it gently from the cutting surface to a plate held just a fraction of an inch below the level of the cutting surface.

If it is a self-serve operation, such as vending or "offer" service in school, college, or industrial feeding, the sandwiches may be cut and wrapped immediately after preparation before storage.

FROSTING

[*10*]   An example of a task that uses a circular motion is the frosting of cupcakes. To do this pick up the cupcake with either hand or both (see Principle 2) and dip the top into the frosting. To flow smoothly, the frosting used in this procedure will need to be a little softer than frosting spread with a spatula.

With a circular motion swirl the cupcake in the frosting. As the cupcake is lifted, another circular motion forms a peak in the frosting on the top. This adds a decorative curl and at the same time eliminates the messy appearance of frosting dribbled down the side of the cupcake.

STIRRING

[*11*]   Another process that uses smooth strokes and is done frequently in foodservice is stirring. The preparing of cooked cereal, gravies, sauces, gelatin, and the reconstituting of fruit juices employ this procedure as a part of the task. Use a smooth, continuous stroke. Avoid a motion in which the direction is sharply changed. Stops and sudden changes in direction make an unnecessary strain on the arm muscles and result in more rapid fatigue. It is less tiring to use a smooth, sweeping stroke.

A smooth, sweeping stroke takes advantage of the momentum developed in the "pull" part of the stroke to assist the arm in doing the more tiring "push" part of the stroke. By using a circular motion, the arm makes smooth, easy strokes.

CUTTING

[*12*]   When cutting celery or slicing carrots with a French knife on a cutting board, use a circular motion. This stroke is really composed of two parts. The first part consists of a downward and forward motion for the cutting operation. The second part of the stroke completes the circle. At the end of the forward stroke lift the heel of the knife and pull it back to the starting position. The heel of the knife and the forearm make a clockwise circle. The point of the knife is moved back and forth without being lifted off the board (Fig. 8).

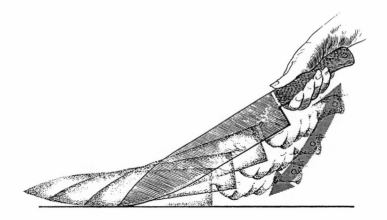

Fig. 8. Circular cutting motion

CHOPPING

[*13*]   When chopping nuts, parsley, or other small pieces, use a stroke that is similar to the one used for cutting and slicing. The chopping stroke is accomplished by holding the point of the knife with the heel of the left hand. The right hand moves the knife up and down and in a quarter-circle on the surface of the cutting board (Fig. 9). (If left-handed reverse the procedure.)

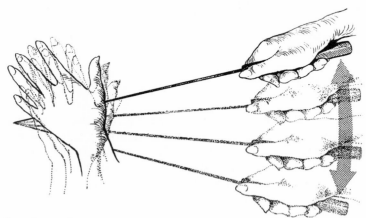

Fig. 9. Chopping stroke

[*14*]   In some cases you may like to use two knives instead of one to further increase the efficiency of chopping. The procedure for using two knives is the same as that described for the use of a single knife. When using two knives, be sure that they are identical so the stroke will be smooth. Identical blades are also necessary to prevent the handles from slipping as the blades touch the board. If the handles slip they may cause a blister on the palm.

LEARNING ACTIVITY

GET READY: Have two opened No. 10 cans of applesauce or pudding to be portioned, a scoop of the size needed to portion the product for your facility, and two rubber scrapers — one large and one small. Serve the product with the scoop removing all the food that can be gotten out easily using the scoop.

DO: **Method I:** After removing the applesauce with the scoop, work as quickly as possible to remove the remaining product by scraping the sides and bottom of the can with a small rubber scraper. Be quite thorough. Record the number of strokes and the amount of time spent. Make note of the amount of product that was removed with the scraper that would have been discarded if the scraper had not been used.

_____strokes _____seconds _____ounces of food

Method II: After removing the food with the scoop, remove the remaining food by scraping the sides and bottom of the can with a large scraper using long, smooth strokes. Record the number of strokes and the amount of time spent. Make note of the amount of food that was removed with the scraper that would have been discarded if the scraper had not been used.

_____strokes _____seconds _____ounces of food

EVALUATE: Which method required the least strokes?_____

How many strokes were saved?_____

Which method required the least time?_____

How much time was saved?_____

Which method saved the most food?_____

How much food was saved?_____

How many cans of food are used in your facility each week in which product is lost by not scraping the can?_____

SUMMARY: Time, energy, and product can be saved if a job is done using rhythmic and smooth-flowing motions.

PRINCIPLE 2 . . .

Make Both Hands Productive at the Same Time

The two hands should work together, beginning and ending motions with both at the same time. The motions of the two hands should be symmetrical and simultaneous. This means that at exactly the same time both hands are performing similar tasks. For example, while the left hand is moving from A to B, the right hand is moving from X to Y (Fig. 10).

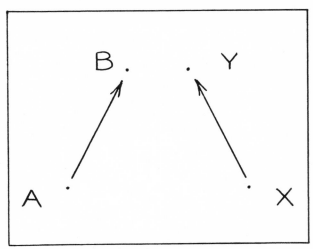

Fig. 10. Symmetrical and simultaneous strokes

19

In many tasks productivity can be doubled by using both hands instead of one. There is less body strain when the hands move symmetrically than when they make nonsymmetrical motions. The symmetrical movements of the arms tend to balance each other.

SALAD MAKING

One task done frequently in foodservice is making salad. Making a pear salad with cherry garnish can be done efficiently or inefficiently. Look at the workers in your kitchen and observe the method they are using. The inefficient method uses only the right hand (left hand if you are left-handed) to do productive work. In the inefficient method the left hand rests on the counter [16] or holds the container of pear halves; the right hand, using a fork, puts a pear half on each plate.

[17]   In the second step of the inefficient method, the left hand rests on the counter or holds the container of cherries and the right hand puts a cherry in the center of each pear half.

By changing from the inefficient to the efficient method we have reduced the equipment used, the distance the hands traveled and the amount of time required to complete the tray of salads.

The efficient method involves use of simultaneous and symmetrical motions, so that both hands may be productive at the same time.

Set the container of pear halves and cherries beside the tray of salad plates and do productive work with both hands. Wearing disposable plastic gloves, pick up two pear halves in each hand. [18] Place one on each salad plate (Fig. 11). Repeat the procedure two more times to place pears on all 12 plates.

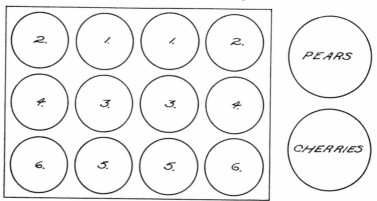

Fig. 11

[*19*]   When all the pear halves have been placed, garnish each with a cherry. Picking up several cherries in each hand, place one in the center of each pear half, working in the same sequence as that used in placing the pear halves.

SANDWICH MAKING

Another task that can be done efficiently while using both hands symmetrically and simultaneously is making grilled cheese sandwiches.

[*20*]   The first step is to butter the tray. There are many acceptable methods of applying butter to the tray. For example, using an 8 oz ladle, spread 8 oz of melted butter, or whatever amount you desire, down the center of an 18 x 26 inch bun pan (Fig. 12).

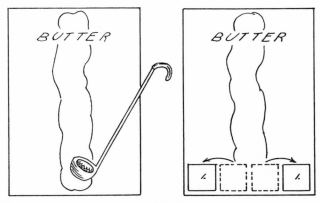

Fig. 12   Fig. 13

[*21*]   The second step is to place the bread on the tray. Pick up four or six slices of bread in each hand. Simultaneously place the bottom slice in each hand on the tray so they touch in the middle and then draw them to the outside edge of the pan (Fig. 13).

This procedure allows these first two slices to be adequately covered with butter, yet leaves enough on the pan for the next two slices. Next place two slices in the middle positions (Fig. 14).

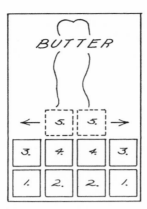

Fig. 14

Fig. 15

This procedure allows the butter to be spread evenly over all four slices with a minimum effort. Continue the same procedure until 24 slices of bread have been placed (Fig. 15).

You may prefer to spread the butter on the pan using a brush, a sprayer, or a paint roller if an exact measurement of butter is not needed. If you need to use exactly 8 oz, or whatever amount you desire, you may pour on a larger amount of butter and tip the pan until all surfaces are covered. Pour off excess butter, leaving 8 oz or desired amount.

[22]   The third step is to place the cheese on the bread. Place stacks of 12 slices of cheese on the No. 6 slices of bread (See Fig. 15). Lift two slices of cheese in each hand and place them on the No. 12 slices of bread. Next with each hand, lift the top slices of cheese from the No. 12 slices of bread and place them on the No. 11 slices of bread.

[23]   Repeat the procedure with two slices of cheese in each hand for the No. 10 and No. 9, No. 8 and No. 7, No. 2 and No. 1, No. 4 and No. 3 pairs. Place the last extra slice in each stack of cheese on the No. 5 slices of bread.

The fourth step is to place a top slice of buttered bread on each sandwich. To do this, first place several ounces of melted [24] butter on a second bun pan. Pick up a slice of bread in each hand and gently pat them in the butter. Place the two slices of [25] bread, butter side up, on any pair of sandwiches. Continue until every sandwich is complete. Add more melted butter to the second bun pan as needed. About 8 oz should be adequate for 24 slices of bread. If you desire more or less butter, make the necessary adjustments. You may prefer to butter the top slice using a brush, sprayer, paint roller, or even a spatula if it can be done without rehandling the slices of bread.

The pan of completed sandwiches should be covered with wax paper and refrigerated to maintain freshness until time for toasting. If you are oven toasting the sandwiches, you may also want to consider applying butter to a second tray and inverting it over the tray of completed sandwiches. This will reduce drying during storage and make the top of the sandwiches look grilled instead of toasted.

They may be toasted either in the oven or on a grill depending on the availability of equipment and time and on personal preference. Toasting should begin just prior to service and continue throughout the serving period to maintain the quality at the highest possible level.

DIPPING IN BATTER

One of the tasks done by cooks and frequently disliked because it is somewhat messy involves dipping food in batter. For example, chicken pieces that will be browned in deep fat and baked in the oven are first dipped in batter.

The first step in preparing to dip chicken in batter is to set up the work area (Fig 16).

Fig. 16

Four pans will be needed: one containing the chicken, one containing the batter, and two empty ones — one to contain the excess batter as it is drained and one to store the chicken. A colander (a large strainer may be used if you prefer) and a deep fat fryer are also required.

Using both hands, pick up several pieces of chicken (8-12 depending on size of equipment) and drop them into a colander that has been set into the container of batter. Be sure each piece of chicken is thoroughly covered. Lift the colander and place on an empty pan to allow surplus batter to drain off.

The chicken may then either be put directly into the deep fat fryer for cooking or into a pan for refrigerator storage until cooking is desired.

BREADING

An arrangement similar to the one used for dipping in batter is used for breading. Veal, pork, turkey, or any other variety of cutlets that will be browned on a grill and baked in the oven are first breaded.

Breading is a two-step procedure as compared to the single-step procedure of dipping in batter. For this reason more equipment and handling are required. The first step in preparing to bread veal cutlets or any other product is to set up the work area with all the needed tools and supplies (Fig 17).

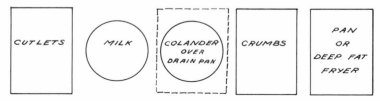

Fig. 17

To do the job, five pans will be needed: one for veal cutlets, one for milk, one for seasoned crumbs, and two empty ones — one to drain milk over and one to hold the breaded cutlets. A colander or large strainer is also needed. People may prefer different types of equipment.

First prepare the seasoned crumbs. This will include all ingredients and seasonings to be used. You may want to include salt, garlic salt, celery salt, salt substitute, seasoned salt, pepper, flour, cornmeal, graham cracker crumbs, and/or dry bread crumbs. Use the combination of these and/or other ingredients in the amount you desire to enhance the product you are preparing.

[26]   Pick up several cutlets using both hands; drop them into the colander that has been set in the milk, being sure they are completely covered; lift the colander and place in pan to drain.

[27]   Pick up one well-drained cutlet in each hand. Lay the cutlets
[28] flat on the crumbs; turn them over so both sides are well covered.

[29]   The cutlets may then be counted into pans so they can be refrigerated until it is time for them to be grilled.

         Hands should not do work that can be done by other parts
[30] of the body. If the necessary adaptations are made to the equipment, the foot or knee can be used to open and close valves on a dishwashing machine, turn water on and off at a sink, and activate or stop a garbage disposal unit. Use of the foot or knee for turning machines on and off frees both hands so they may do productive work.

LEARNING ACTIVITY

GET READY: Set up several trays of salads or desserts that have been preportioned and transferred to plates or dishes. Get a tray stand or cart and be ready to work behind the serving counter.

DO: **Method I:** Using one hand, hold the tray of salads or desserts with one end supported on the counter. With the other hand, transfer the salads or desserts from the tray to the serving counter, arranging them as you would for service. Record the number transferred in one minute using only one hand to do productive work.

_____dishes transferred in one minute.

Method II: Place the tray of salads or desserts on a tray stand or cart. Using both hands in parallel motions, pick up two salads or desserts, one in each hand, and transfer them from the tray to the serving counter. Record the number transferred in one minute using with hands.

_____dishes transferred in one minute.

EVALUATE: Which method was used to transfer more salads or desserts in one minute?_____

How many more were transferred in one minute using that method?_____

How many preportioned servings of salad, fruit, dessert, etc. are served in your facility each day?_____ Each week?_____ Each month?_____

To further understand the importance of this, divide the number served in your facility each week by the difference between the number transferred by the two methods. This is the number of minutes that would be wasted weekly by someone in your facility by using the inefficient method.

_____minutes would be wasted weekly.

Now multiply this by the hourly wage of the person doing the work.

_____dollars difference between the two methods.

SUMMARY: Time, energy, and money can be saved if a job is done efficiently by using both hands at the same time to do productive work.

PRINCIPLE 3 . . .

Make Hand and Body Motions Few, Short, and Simple

Each motion should use the least possible time and energy. When it is possible to accomplish a task by using a hand motion, it is inefficient to use the whole arm. When it is possible to accomplish a task by an arm motion, it is inefficient to use a reach that requires the whole body to move or turn.

BISCUITS

One example in which motions could be conserved might be
[32] in the cutting of biscuits. Biscuits are traditionally worked on a
[33] floured breadboard. The dough is rolled out with a rolling pin to
[34] the desired thickness. It is then cut with a biscuit cutter or a
[35] similar round tool. The biscuits are picked up from the floured
[36] board and transferred to a baking sheet. The scrap is then rerolled and recut. These recut biscuits are less desirable products because of the additional handling.
[37] Even though some people may think the product not quite as attractive, efficiency is increased if the dough is rolled out directly on the bun pan. Weigh out the dough needed to make the correct number of desired size biscuits. For example, to make 60 biscuits that are each ½ oz, weigh out 30 oz of dough. Roll
[38] the dough into a rectangular shape in the pan, pushing it into the corners as necessary. To shape the biscuits, cut the dough
[39] into squares, diamonds, or any other shape. Use a knife, a long

27

spatula, or a dough cutter instead of a round biscuit cutter. As the cuts are made to shape the biscuits, the dough will separate so that browning will be even.

This method has several advantages. It requires less time and fewer motions, reduces the scrap, saves reworking and rerolling the dough, and results in a more tender product. It also eliminates the job of transferring the rolls or biscuits from the cutting board to the baking sheet. To check on the saving of time, compare the time required for the two methods.

KNIVES

[40]   Knives should be stored in a knife rack (Fig 18) to prevent dulling of the blades and injury to the people handling them. Ready accessibility also saves time and motion.

Fig. 18. Knife rack

It would be ideal to have a small rack for storing the knives used in each production area: paring, French, and fruit knives in the salad area; paring and French knives in the vegetable preparation area; boning, slicing, paring, and French knives in the cooks' area; fruit and utility knives in the serving area; and so on.

When cutting cakes, frozen salads, or desserts use a case knife or table knife to avoid scratching the pan. Dip the knife in hot water before each stroke to make a smooth cut. This will make the knife pull more easily and reduce the ragged edges that result if a dry knife is used.

RECIPES

[41]   Standardized recipes are necessary for production control and portion control. It is important to use standardized recipes that include the size of pan and the number of portions per pan.
[42] An exact yield from a recipe will result if the correct amount is put into the right size pan and cut into the correct number of equal-sized portions. In some cases, it may be desirable to cut smaller portions for children or people with small appetites. If this is so, it should be by plan rather than by accident. The size of the portions of food should not depend on the ability of the person doing the cutting. If the equipment budget permits, a marker should be purchased. However, a fast, effective system is to mark the rim of the pan with a scratch.

MEASUREMENTS

It may be necessary to increase or decrease a recipe according to the amount of product needed. This table of equivalent measures should be helpful in assisting you in this job.

$$3 \text{ tsp} = 1 \text{ T}$$
$$4 \text{ T} = \frac{1}{4} \text{ c}$$
$$16 \text{ T} = 1 \text{ c}$$
$$2 \text{ c} = 1 \text{ pt}$$
$$4 \text{ c} = 1 \text{ qt}$$
$$4 \text{ qt} = 1 \text{ gal}$$
$$16 \text{ oz} = 1 \text{ lb}$$

Both efficiency and food quality will be improved by selection of the correct measuring tool for each recipe ingredient.

Using the following recipe for meat loaf, list each ingredient in the amount that could be measured and the tool that would be the most appropriate for measuring the ingredient with the greatest efficiency (answers on page 36).

Most Efficient Measure

6 lb ground beef	. . . .
5 c dry bread crumbs	. . . .
4 c milk	. . . .
3 eggs	. . . .
8 T catsup	. . . .
¼ qt chopped onions	. . . .
6 tsp salt	. . . .
½ tsp pepper	. . . .

Now double this recipe for meat loaf. Select the tool or tools which would most efficiently measure each of the ingredients (answers on page 36).

Single Amount	*Most Efficient Measure* *Double Amount*
6 lb ground beef	. . . .
5 c dry bread crumbs	. . . .
1 qt milk	. . . .
3 eggs	. . . .
½ c catsup	. . . .
1 c chopped onions	. . . .
2 T salt	. . . .
½ tsp pepper	. . . .

Less time is required for measuring when the correct tool is used. To check this theory, compare the time required to measure one-half cup of catsup and 8 T of catsup.

[*43*]   More accuracy is achieved by measuring with the correct tool. To check this theory, measure 8 T of catsup into a one-half cup measure. It should be level full; however, materials like catsup tend to round up in the measure, and 8 T will yield more than one-half cup.

[*44*]   If a scale is available, measuring by weight rather than measure is preferable for both speed and accuracy. To check this theory, have three different people measure a level cup of brown sugar, firmly packed. Weigh the three cupfuls of brown sugar and compare the three weights.

PIES

[*45*]   Pie is one of the most difficult foods to portion evenly unless a marker (Fig. 19) is used.

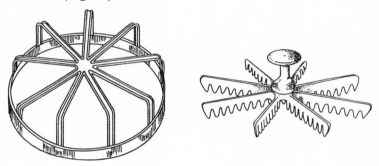

Fig. 19. Pie markers

With practice and a good eye, it is possible to become quite proficient at cutting a pie into eight equal portions, but if a smaller pie pan is used so that a serving is one-seventh of the pie, or a larger one is used so that it is cut into nine pieces, equal portions are very difficult without a marker.

Many varieties of markers are available. If your facility serves pie frequently, it would be of value to invest in a marker so that each portion would be exactly the same size.

The first step in serving pie is to assemble all the needed supplies: pie, marker, knife, pie spatula, dessert plates, and trays.

The second step is to mark the pies. To avoid multiple handling, mark several pies before laying down the marker.

The next step is to cut the pies. One good method is to cut completely across the pie in one stroke. Then turn it a quarter turn and cut completely across it again. Each of the quarters is then cut in half (Fig. 20).

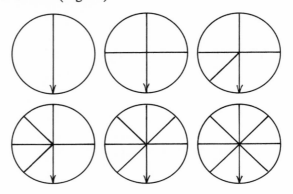

Fig. 20. Pie cut crust to crust

A particularly good method for cutting cream and meringue pies is to start from the center and cut to the edge eight times. Turn the pan one-eighth turn between each cut (Fig. 21).

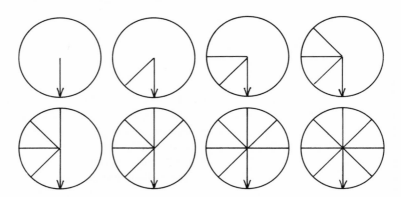

Fig. 21. Pie cut center to crust

When all the pies have been cut, place the first one just to one side of an empty tray and in front of two stacks of dessert plates (Fig. 22).

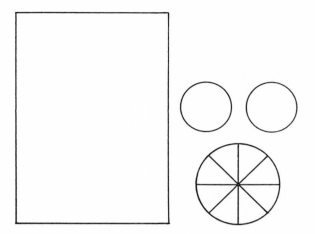

Fig. 22

Or you may place the cut pie just to one side of the tray of empty dessert plates (Fig. 23).

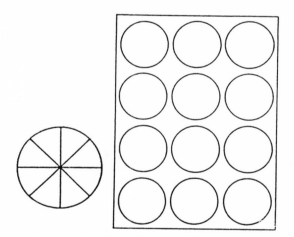

Fig. 23

[46]   Using the pie spatula (Fig. 24), lift the outside edge of one piece and slide the spatula to the center. Lift the pie out and place it on a dessert plate. Follow the same procedure for the second piece.

Fig. 24. Pie spatula

[47]   Lift the remaining six pieces by sliding the spatula from the point to the edge (Fig. 25). This procedure protects the point from being broken and makes use of the side of the pie pan to prevent the piece of pie from sliding while the spatula is being pushed under it.

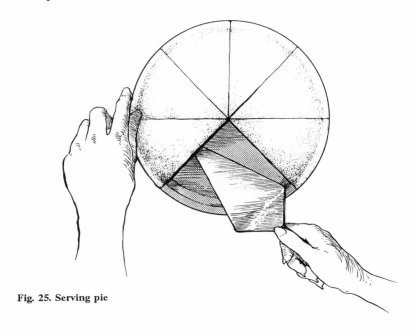

Fig. 25. Serving pie

LEARNING ACTIVITY

GET READY: Prepare a meatball mixture accord to your preferred recipe. Get several bun pans, a scoop of the size needed to produce the desired portion, a sheet of parchment paper, a plate or hamburger press. Scoop 40 portions onto each of three pans and be ready to make them into patties using each of three methods.

DO: Method I: Pick up the patties one at a time in your hands and shape them with your hands and place them again on the pan.

Time required to shape 40 patties?_____minutes

Method II: Shape the patties by pressing them with a plate or hamburger press without lifting them from the pan.

Time required to shape 40 patties?_____minutes

Method III: Shape the patties by pressing all of them at the same time with a second pan, using a parchment sheet to keep the meat from sticking to the bottom of the upper pan.

Time required to shape 40 patties?_____minutes

EVALUATE: Which method required the least time?_____

What was the difference in time between the least efficient and the most efficient methods? _____

How often does your facility have meat patties? _____ times per week

Based on the quantity you prepare each time, what savings in time would there be if this amount were made for your needs. Determine this by dividing the amount you use by 40 and then multiply that number by the difference in time determined above.

_____minutes would be saved.

Divide by 60 to find the hours saved.

_____hours would be saved.

Multiply this by the hourly wage of the person doing the work.

_____dollars saved using the efficient method.

SUMMARY: Time, energy, and money can be saved if a job is done efficiently by making both hands productive at the same time.

MEAT LOAF ANSWERS

Most efficient single measure	*Most efficient double measure*
6 lb ground beef	12 lb ground beef
1 qt + 1 c crumbs	2½ qt crumbs
1 qt milk	2 qt milk
3 eggs	6 eggs
½ c catsup	1 c catsup
1 c chopped onions	2 c chopped onions
2 T salt	¼ c salt
½ tsp pepper	1 tsp pepper

PRINCIPLE 4 . . .

Maintain Comfortable Working Positions and Conditions

The most important single piece of equipment used in accomplishing work is the body. Some understanding of the mechanics of your body will help you use it more effectively. When your spine is held straight, the muscles can maintain good posture with a minimum of strain and effort whether you are working, sitting, standing, or walking.

CHAIRS

[49]   A chair that is the correct height allows a person to sit with hips and knees at right angles and feet flat on the floor. A chair that is too low makes it necessary for the person to sit without benefit of thighs to support part of the body weight and to provide balance.

[50]   A chair that is too high will be uncomfortable in one of two ways. If the person sits with her feet on the floor, she is only perched on the edge of the seat; on folding chairs this is dangerous as well as uncomfortable. If she sits squarely on the seat to use the back support, her legs will dangle. Circulation is often restricted in this position, which if continued for a period of time may cause one or both legs to "go to sleep."

WORK SURFACES

Selecting the proper height for work surfaces is an additional help in maintaining good posture.

[51]   To find the proper work height for mixing and beating, stand comfortably erect in front of the table with arms straight and press your hands flat on the table top (Fig. 26). The proper work height for mixing and beating could also be determined by

[52] measuring from the wrist to the floor. The proper work height allows a person to mix or stir without raising the forearm above the elbow. It is very tiring to work when the forearm is higher than the elbow.

Fig. 26. Proper height for work surfaces

[53]   To find the proper table height for working with small hand tools, stand erect with your arm hanging comfortably by your

[54] side. The table height should be 4 inches below the elbow. Have someone help by measuring from the elbow to the floor. From the number subtract 4 inches to find the proper table height for working with small tools.

This is the best table height when using a French knife and making sandwiches and salads. It will allow work to be done comfortably without raising the hands above the elbows. There will probably be several table heights in the kitchen from which to chose. It may be necessary to make adjustments if none of the work surfaces are the correct height. If the work surface is too high, this may be corrected by altering the length of the table legs. Or it may be necessary to find another surface. Perhaps a utility cart could provide a surface of the correct height.

[55] If the work surface is too low, it is easy to put extensions on the legs of the table. For a quick and easy solution, place an inverted baking sheet or a large cutting board on the surface of the table.

MOVEMENT

Changing your position will prove restful when it is necessary for you to stand or sit in one place for a long period. The basic position of the body should be one that is comfortably erect not only when standing and sitting but also during activity.

In addition to correct counter and chair heights, other factors concerning the workplace need to be considered.

ILLUMINATION

Good illumination is the first requirement for satisfactory vision. Good lighting lessens eyestrain and fatigue. It reduces the number of errors in recipe reading. It helps see food soil that is accidentally left on dishes and pans. It also helps prevent errors
[56] in reading gauges and thermometers. Light in the kitchen should range from 15 footcandles on the floor to 35 footcandles on equipment and 35–50 footcandles on work surfaces.

It is unlikely that your facility will have the equipment

necessary to make the measurement, but most power companies will be willing to visit you and measure the amount of light. At your request they will suggest ways in which the lighting can be improved.

Light-colored, smooth ceilings and walls reflect light better than dark or porous surfaces. Changing a ceiling or wall surface from a dark color to a lighter one may improve the light in the room. Care must be taken to avoid having walls that are too smooth because the glare from the shiny surface can be tiring.

In addition to improving vision, a light, airy room soon improves morale and makes the whole work experience more enjoyable. A room that is light-colored and well-lighted would be more pleasant to work in than a dark-colored, poorly lighted room.

VENTILATION

[57]   When planning a workplace that will be comfortable, ventilation is important. The air should be changed approximately every five minutes. This is a factor that will require the attention of an engineer, but even an untrained person can distinguish between a room in which the air has been circulating and a poorly ventilated room that has been closed several hours.

TEMPERATURE

[58]   Temperature for food preparation and service areas should be maintained at 75–80° F (Fig. 27). Higher temperatures will cause the heart rate to increase and fatigue will occur sooner. Hoods over cooking equipment draw off much of the excess heat and odor from the source. They should be kept clean for operation at full efficiency as well as for sanitation and safety reasons.

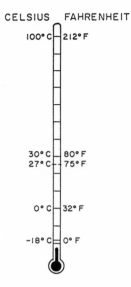

Fig. 27. Thermometer

HUMIDITY

[*59*]   Relative humidity should be maintained at 50–60 percent. Higher humidity lowers productivity and increases fatigue. Lower humidity causes exposed surfaces of food to dry out too quickly. Air conditioning is almost a necessity where the weather is hot and humid during the summer months. If this is not possible, a good fan and exhaust system may serve the purpose.

NOISE

[*60*]   Noise and vibration have a disturbing and tiring effect on most people. Mistakes occur more often in a noisy kitchen that in a quiet one. Control of the noise level is possible through use of sound-absorbing ceiling materials, smooth-running motors, and mobile equipment with neoprene wheels. It is also important to train employees to work quietly.

FLOORS

[*61*]   Floors that are resilient are less tiring than hard floors when people are standing for extended periods. If the job a person is doing requires standing in the same general area for a long time each day, it might be worthwhile to purchase special cushioned shoes to help reduce fatigue.

LEARNING ACTIVITY

GET READY: Have a tape measure or measuring stick at least 4 feet long and someone to assist you.

DO: **Surface I:** To find the proper work height for mixing and beating, stand comfortably erect and look straight ahead. Have a helper measure from the heel of your hand to the floor.

What is the work height that you found correct for you to use?_____inches

Is there a work surface of this height already in your area?_____

If not, what will you do to make your surface the correct height?_____

_____

Surface II: To find the proper table height for working with small hand tools, stand comfortably erect and look straight ahead. Have the helper measure from your elbow to the floor and subtract 4 inches.

What is the table height that you found correct for working with small hand tools?_____inches

Is there a work surface of this height already in your work area?_____

If not, what will you do to make your surface the correct height?_____

EVALUATE: How many work surfaces do you work on each day?_____

How many inches of adjustment are required? _____ inches

Is it more comfortable working on counter heights that are correct?_____

SUMMARY: Work is done more easily and fatigue reduced when correct counter heights are used and comfortable working positions are maintained.

PRINCIPLE 5 . . .

Locate Materials for Efficient Sequence of Motions

Arrangement of supplies and equipment in the work area is particularly important where a single activity requiring a short time takes place repeatedly.

SETTING UP TRAYS

One of the best examples of this is in the setting up of trays. In this activity the arrangement of the workplace can make the difference between confusion and efficiency. To set up trays in an efficient manner, arrange the work area as shown in Figure 28.

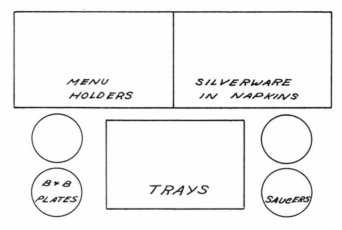

Fig. 28. Tray setup area

43

FIRST, place a stack of trays on the work area directly in front
of the worker. Other items will be moved from their location
to a position on the tray.

[63] SECOND, place a tray of wrapped silverware on a shelf above
and to the right of the work area. If no shelf is available,
place it on a cart to the right of the worker.

[64] THIRD, place a tray of condiment and menu holders in a shelf
above and to the left of the work area. If no shelf is available, place it on a cart to the left of the worker.

FOURTH, place bread and butter plates in a stack or two to the
left of the trays. If a large number of trays are to be set up,
it would be desirable to locate a cart of plates in that position so
they may be taken directly from the cart rather than rehandling
them.

FINALLY, place saucers in a stack to the right of the trays. As
with the bread and butter plates it may be better to use a
cart that holds saucers. If desired, cups might also be placed on
the tray at this point.

Set up the tray as shown in Figure 29. Using Principle 2,
work with both hands at the same time; do not pass items from
one hand to the other. It takes twice as long to handle the item
twice as to pick up the item and place it on the tray with the
same hand. Reach with the right hand to pick up the wrapped
silverware and with the left hand to pick up the filled condiment
holder that holds the menu. Place both on the tray at the same
time.

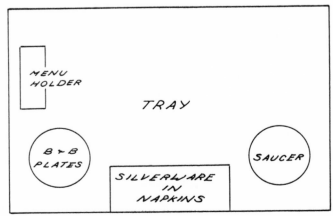

Fig. 29. Tray arrangement

Reach with the right hand to pick up the saucer and with the left hand to pick up the bread and butter plate. Place both things on the tray at the same time.

The activities just described can be the responsibility of one person on a serving line that uses several people. Be sure there is a balance of work load for everyone on the serving line. If any one person is responsible for putting too many things on the tray, she will detain everyone else. The serving line can move only as fast as the slowest person working on that line.

[65]

In small facilities trays may be filled by two or three people or in two or three steps. Trays may be set up as just described, combined with the serving of chilled foods such as salads, desserts, and bread and butter as the first step. If the person setting up the trays adds chilled items, they all should be located in easy reach so that each hand can grasp an item at the same time.

A tray rack 20 × 27 inches is available in several heights. It can be used to hold trays of special desserts, wrapped bread, wrapped crackers, butter pats, etc. After these items are in place, the hot food can be added by a second person.

BREAKING DOWN TRAYS

A similar task that also illustrates the importance of having supplies and equipment located to permit the best sequence is the breaking down of the tray when it is returned after the meal. It is possible to operate efficiently with less than ideal in equipment and layout.

DISHWASHING SETUP

An ideal dishwashing setup would include a soiled-dish table, a soak sink, a dish-return window, a garbage disposal, a slanted overhead shelf, a dishwashing machine, a clean-dish table, and ample floor space (Fig. 30).

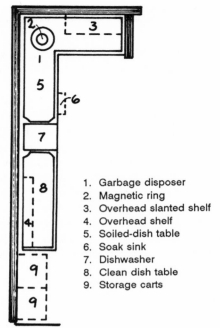

1. Garbage disposer
2. Magnetic ring
3. Overhead slanted shelf
4. Overhead shelf
5. Soiled-dish table
6. Soak sink
7. Dishwasher
8. Clean dish table
9. Storage carts

Fig. 30. Ideal dishwashing setup

THE SOILED-DISH TABLE should be long enough to allow 3 or 4 feet of work surface for scraping the dishes before the garbage disposal unit. Between the garbage disposal unit and the dishwashing machine there should be room for at least two racks. A soiled-dish table that is not adequate in length can be supplemented with a cart pulled into position for the time it is needed.

[66] **THE SOAK SINK** should be portable for maximum efficiency. It could be a small dishpan placed on a cart; a fabricated unit of stainless steel with a drain; or any of several intermediate types of material, style, cost, and convenience.

[67] **THE DISH-RETURN WINDOW** may be necessary in a facility where the dining room is adjacent to the dish room. It provides a means of transporting soiled dishes from the dining room to the dish room.

If there are soiled dishes coming from two sources, such as the main dining room and a banquet room, a cart could be used to store the dining room dishes while the others are being processed.

THE GARBAGE DISPOSAL UNIT should be installed in the soiled-dish table. It should be placed far enough from the dishwashing machine to avoid cross-traffic. A disposal unit always has a water source. For maximum efficiency, be sure that it is installed and maintained so that the spray nozzle is 15 to 20 inches above the table. The water may be controlled either by a foot pedal or a clamp so that both hands are free to work.

A disposal unit could be replaced by a conveniently located waste container if necessary. In many cases the waste container can be placed under the hole in the soiled-dish table, in which the disposal unit will eventually be installed. If losing flatware in the disposal unit or waste container is a problem, it may be helpful to install a magnetic ring that will salvage pieces of flatware that are accidentally thrown away with food and paper waste.

[68] THE SLANTED OVERHEAD SHELF should be installed over the soiled-dish table. It should be 20 inches wide with a rim along the front edge and, if possible, with a gutter and drain in the lower angle. It should be installed 15 inches above the dish table and placed at a 20° angle. It is preferable that the overhead shelf be long enough for at least two racks, but depending on the space available, it can be 20, 40, or 60 inches in length.

Many people think of machines and automation as labor eliminators. Machines in our modern times are "labor serving" rather than "labor saving" or "labor eliminating." They supplement hand labor by performing the tasks that are disagreeable or hazardous.

THE MECHANICAL DISHWASHER makes it possible to eliminate the disagreeable task of hand washing dishes, which necessitates having hands in hot water for long periods, as well as the hazardous task of sanitizing the dishes in water that is 180° to 190° F.

[69] THE CLEAN-DISH TABLE should be long enough to hold at least four racks. The clean-dish table can be extended by the use of carts and dish dispensers. They can be conveniently arranged around the person unloading the dishwashing machine to reduce walking to a minimum.

[70] **LIGHTWEIGHT PLASTIC RACKS** for washing and storing cups and glasses reduce the handling of each of these items. In fact, because of the open construction, these racks can be removed as soon as they emerge from the machine. The drying will take place on the rack instead of taking up valuable space on the clean-dish table.

Ample floor space should be allowed at the clean end of the dishwashing machine for several carts. The racks can be put directly onto the cart that will be moved to the point of use.

If any of the features discussed here are missing from your dishwashing setup and it is possible to add one or more, the addition would be an improvement. Other types of arrangements are necessary for flight-type dishwashing machines. There are many ways equipment can be arranged to make an efficient dishwashing operation.

LEARNING ACTIVITY

GET READY: Get permission from the supervisor and the server who is to be observed. Get a stopwatch or have a conveniently located large clock with a second hand.

DO: Observe the person who is serving the main dish on the serving line. Make a sketch showing the location of all items that are handled by the server. Time the serving of 10 plates.

Is the plate dispenser located conveniently to the left of the server?_____

Are the plates removed from the dispenser one at a time as needed to avoid rehandling and working around a stack of plates on the counter?_____

Are the foods located in a logical pattern so no back-tracking is required, for example, to put on a gravy or sauce?_____

Are the items used most often brought to the table in large pans to reduce refilling or replenishing items?_____

Are the items that might drip (gravy or vegetables in liquid) placed so they will not accidentally dribble into another container as they are being served?_____

Are the most frequently used items in the most easily reached locations to avoid many long reaches?_____

Is the garnish last, so it can be added after all other items are in place?_____

If these questions and others show that some changes need to be made to improve efficiency, make the suggestions to your supervisor. Request that the changes be made to test your theory and that they allow you to time the serving of 10 plates using the revised operation. It would be even better if your new method could be practiced several times to improve proficiency before the process is timed.

EVALUATE:　Were some changes made to improve efficiency?
_____

Was time saved after the system was revised?
_____

How much time was saved for each 10 plates served?_____

Did the server accept your suggestions?_____

As you began making changes were other problems observed?_____

SUMMARY: Time and energy can be saved if materials are located for an efficient sequence of motions.

Use the Best Available Equipment for the Job

Regardless of how well equipped the kitchen in which you work is, your job will be made easier by understanding how each piece of equipment is operated, cleaned, and maintained. Every kitchen contains equipment; a few have the finest possible, and a few have only the bare minimum. Most kitchens are somewhere between these two extremes.

PREPARATION EQUIPMENT

When cooking, select the most efficient piece of equipment available for the job to be done. For example, macaroni could be cooked in a double boiler or a steam-jacketed kettle.

DOUBLE BOILER. If a double boiler is used, be sure it is in good condition and sits squarely on the stove. A pan that is large enough to cover the entire burner provides maximum use of available heat (Fig. 31). Have the flame adjusted properly. The tip of the flame should just touch the bottom of the pan. Flames that come up around the edge of the

Fig. 31. Double boiler

51

pan not only waste heat but also make the pan unnecessarily dirty.

[72] **STEAM-JACKETED KETTLE.** If you have a steam-jacketed kettle, be sure the steam supply is adequate and that you know how to operate it correctly.

Be sure whatever container you chose is in good repair and sanitary. Choose equipment of the proper size to handle the amount of product being prepared.

If a double broiler is used, it is important to know the capacities of the available pans and to select the one that will be filled to two-thirds capacity by the amount of food being prepared. It may be helpful to mark capacity levels on the inside of the pan with a scratch. To do this, put a quart (or gallon, depending on size) of water in the pan and scratch a line at the depth. Add another quart (or gallon) and scratch another line at that depth. Continue to the desired depth.

If a steam-jacketed kettle is available, it should not be filled to a level higher than the jacket, or approximately two-thirds of capacity.

Capacity measures are available for the various brands and sizes of kettles. The most reliable and convenient is the model with the markings etched on the inside. Another model is a ladle that has capacity markings on the handle. By being a ladle, it is a dual purpose tool that can also be used for dipping food out of the kettle. Another model has a strip that is attached to the inside of the kettle to indicate the amount of food in it.

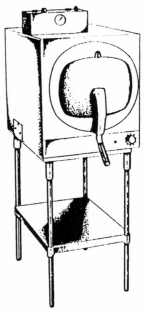

A HIGH-PRESSURE STEAMER operates at 12–15 lb of pressure and is one of the most versatile pieces of equipment in any kitchen (Fig. 32). It is excellent for thawing and quickly cooking frozen vegetables; also for cooking rice, potatoes, beef stew,

Fig. 32. High-pressure steamer

scrambled eggs, poached eggs, soft-cooked eggs, and hard-cooked eggs.

[73]   Hard-cooked eggs that are to be chopped for salads and sandwiches may be broken and shells removed before cooking in the steamer. Much less time is required for this method of preparation than would be needed to peel the same amount of hard-cooked eggs for egg salad sandwiches.

A COMPARTMENT STEAMER operates at 5 lb of pressure and is a good choice for cooking large quantities of foods such as potatoes, pasta, or rice and for reheating food (Fig. 33). Atmospheric convection steamers are pressureless. They cook efficiently because of the fans that move the layer of cold air away from the product and replace it with steam. This system has the advantage of allowing the operators to open the door and check the cooking progress as needed.

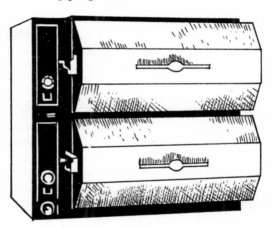

Fig. 33. Compartment steamer

COMBINATION STEAMER/OVENS might be considered in a small kitchen where space is at a premium (Fig. 34). They can operate as either a steamer or an oven; or as a steam-injected oven. This combination feature is great for specialty items such as French bread. The biggest disadvantage is cost. They are almost as expensive as the two pieces purchased separately.

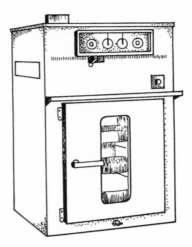

Fig. 34. Combination steamer/oven

If there is either a high-pressure steamer or a compartment steamer not being used in a kitchen it is probably for one of two reasons: It is improperly installed and is not functioning correctly, or there have been no instructions and demonstrations of its use. In either case the salesperson, if known, or the factory should be notified.

[74] **BLENDERS AND FOOD PROCESSORS** may be used to assist in the preparation of many foods. In some facilities, they are used to blend food for infant, liquid, or geriatric diets. They might also be used to chop nuts or cranberries, to blend ingredients for sauces and gravies, and to prepare salad dressing. If a new blender or food processor is to be purchased, request a heavy-duty model. The lightweight or home-style models are not able to stand the amount of wear they will receive when used regularly for large quantities of food.

Food processors should be purchased according to the kind and volume of product to be prepared. The cooks will transfer those tasks they discover or are shown can be done more easily and better on the new equipment. Additional blades and attachments may be added as more uses are discovered.

[75] **CARTS.** Wheels are great muscle and energy savers (Fig. 35). If a container is placed on a cart, it can be rolled to the point of use with much less energy than would be required to carry the

same quantity and weight of material. The larger diameter wheels provide a smoother ride and require less energy to move.

Fig. 35. Utility cart

A strong utility cart can be used as a receiving table for checking in small items and then for transporting them to points of storage or use. Be sure when placing your order that you check the capacity the cart will carry. Even stainless steel will bend if more weight is placed on the shelves than the cost is made to carry.

Use a cart for bringing supplies from the storeroom for the whole day rather than making many trips to get items one at a time. Use a cart to take all the cooked food from the preparation area to the serving line at once instead of making many trips with separate items.

Be sure the bumpers are selected according to need. Wraparound bumpers provide the best protection but are the most expensive and may be more than needed. Donut bumpers guard the corners and are less expensive but will not protect against blows to the middle of the sides and the ends.

Use bins on casters for flour and sugar to eliminate need for the many trips to the storeroom that would be necessary to refill the counter-top canisters. Less effort is required to move this type of bin into proper working position than to pull out heavy built-in bins.

Be very sure that if portable equipment is available it is being used to take full advantage of its mobility and is not treated as if it were stationary.

Energy is used to set the cart in motion, but to keep it going requires very little effort on the part of the person pushing it. Be sure the wheels on the carts are cleaned and oiled regularly. More energy is required to push carts that have dirty and unoiled wheels.

SERVING TOOLS

Serving large quantities of food requires that adequate tools are available and that the employees have knowledge of how to use, maintain, and store them properly. Tools must be the right type and size, of heavy-duty construction, in good repair, and clean. Store them where they are to be used. For example, serving tools should be stored as close as possible to the serving area. The same is true for salad preparation tools and baking tools. Keep both the storage area and the work area as orderly as possible. It is much easier to work when tools and supplies are returned to their regular storage place where they may be quickly located the next time.

Be sure to select the best tool for the job to be done. Use a French whip to combine starch and liquid without having lumps in the cooked product. Use a fruit knife to remove peel from oranges. Use a serrated knife to slice bread, rolls, and buns. Use a boning knife to bone a ham.

KNIVES must be kept sharp. Carbon steel blades usually will take and hold a sharper edge than stainless steel. Check to be sure knives are constructed with through tang, which means the shank of the blade extends the entire length of the handle and is held in place by three rivets.

Store knives away from other utensils to protect the blades and to help avoid accidents. A stainless steel knife holder that can be attached to the end of a work table is a safe, convenient way to store knives. A model that has a removable plate and is open at the bottom is easy to sanitize. Magnets may be mounted for holding knives, but there is more chance for injury with this type of holder than with an enclosed one.

[76]   A French knife
(Fig. 36) has a wide
blade and a handle
that is recessed from

Fig. 36. French knife

the cutting edge. Use a French knife and cutting board for
chopping celery, onions, parsley, nuts, etc., or for slicing onions,
oranges, or tomatoes.

A logical companion for a French knife is a cutting board.
Select one that is nonporous and not too heavy to handle. Hard-
rubber composition boards are available in varying sizes and
thickness. Keep the board meticulously clean.

When chopping or slicing, place the board so that the
product will drop from the board into the container that will be
used for cooking or mixing. This is called drop-delivery and can
be arranged either by placing the cutting board over part of the
pan or by placing the board at the edge of the counter with the
pan next to it on a lower surface.

Slicers may be 10–16 inches in length. Ham slicers are
shorter than roast beef slicers, but a medium length could be
used for either job.

A paring knife is used for removing spots and cutting away
the outer surface of fruits and vegetables. The blade is 3–4
inches long and approximately the same width as the handle.

[77]   A vegetable peeler has two blades that operate as a pair. It
has knee action, which means that the blades rotate on a
common axis. It is used when it is necessary to pare small
amounts of food.

Be sure to sharpen the knife before and during the slicing
operation so that the sharpest possible edge may be maintained.

[78] **SPOONS.** Solid, perforated, and slotted spoons are used for both
cooking and serving (Fig. 37). Solid spoons may be used for
serving products such as squash, stuffed peppers, or casserole
dishes and other foods that are served with the sauce in which
they are cooked. Slotted and perforated spoons should be used
in serving foods such as peas, corn, or asparagus that are served
without liquid but are more attractive when held in steam table
pans with liquid over them to prevent drying. To avoid the
possibility of being burned by a hot handle, use spoons with
insulated handles.

Spoons are available in several lengths. For preparing small amounts in small pans, a short-handled spoon is less likely to cause the pan to tip and spill. When stirring food in deep pots, long-handled spoons help to avoid burns. Be sure to select one of the proper length for the job at hand.

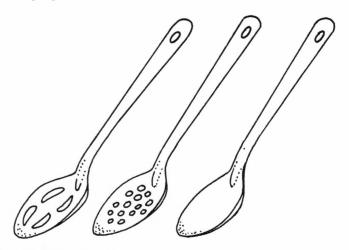

Fig. 37. Slotted, perforated, and solid spoons

A spoodle is a measuring spoon or combination spoon and ladle. They are available in several sizes and are used to serve measured amounts of food. They are, like spoons, available either solid or perforated and in a variety of handle lengths. The stainless steel varieties usually have insulated handles. The polypropylene ones do not absorb heat so do not need special handles.

[79] **WIRE WHIPS** are very efficient when stirring foods, such as gravies and sauces, which have a tendency to lump (Fig. 38). Each wire is a cutting edge, so the whip offers many times the efficiency of a spoon. Whips are available in several weights. Fine piano wire whips may be used for incorporating air into egg whites and cream or for stirring very thin liquids. French whips, which are made of medium weight wire, are used for stirring other light- to medium-viscosity products. Heavy wire is needed for whips used in stirring heavy batters, roux, and sauces. Whips are available in a variety of lengths. The most desirable length will depend on the amount of material and the size of container.

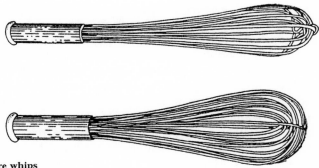

Fig. 38. Wire whips

[*80*] **SPATULAS.** Metal spatulas are available in a variety of lengths
       and widths (Fig. 39). They can be straight or bent. A long,
flexible, straight spatula may be used when frosting cakes. A
short spatula with a blade 1½ inches wide and 4 inches long may
be used to spread butter, mayonnaise, or soft fillings on sandwiches. A spatula with a bend just below the handle may be used
for serving sheet cakes and gelatin salads. Select one that is the
same width as the portion of product being served. Special
pointed spatulas with a bend just below the handle are available
for serving pie and layer cake.

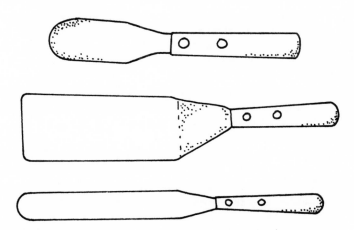

Fig. 39. Metal spatulas

SCRAPERS. Rubber scrapers are the most efficient aid in avoiding loss of product when transferring it from one container to another. Crescent-shaped scrapers made of hard rubber or neoprene are used for cleaning out steam-jacketed kettles and mixer bowls. Large, oblong, hard-rubber scrapers may be used for cleaning food out of large containers such as No. 10 cans and full-size steam table pans. Small rubber scrapers that are 2 × 3¼ inches oblong will efficiently scrape small containers such as small cans and pans. Scrapers with narrow blades 1 × 2¾ inches may be used for cleaning out bottles with narrow mouths, such as those used for catsup and baby food. When using any scraper, make long, even strokes working from the high side to the draining point for maximum efficiency.

MEASURING CUPS AND SPOONS of the largest possible size consistent with the amount of product being measured provide the fastest, most accurate method. For example, measure 4 tsp as 1 T + 1 tsp; measure 1 qt rather than 4 c. Use a measuring cup for measuring and transferring an exact amount of pie filling or cake batter from the mixing bowl to the baking pans.

SCALES are much more accurate than measuring cups or spoons and result in greater consistency of the finished product. Select the scale according to the amount of product to be measured. The accuracy of a small amount such as 3 oz will be improved if weighed on a scale with a maximum of 5 lb rather than on one with a maximum of 50 lb or 100 lb. This may necessitate having at least two scales. One with a large capacity to be located in the receiving area to weigh cases of fruits and vegetables and bags of potatoes and onions. One with a small capacity to be located in the ingredient room to weigh small amounts of ingredients for recipes.

TONGS are available in several lengths and styles. The most popular style for food handling are pom tongs. They may be either 6, 9, or 12 inches long and constructed of stainless steel, aluminum, or polypropylene. They are useful in serving preportioned meat, ear corn, spinach, rolls, relishes, and ice. They are efficient and easy to use because they can be operated easily with one hand. The natural spring, which is a result of the construction, allows the food to be released by relaxing the tension.

SCISSORS work more efficiently than knives in some instances, for they are actually two knives. They are particularly handy for cutting dates, marshmallows, and other sticky foods; for cutting meat and vegetables; for salads; and for preparing bite-sized pieces of food for those who require them.

EGG SLICERS may be used for slicing hard-cooked eggs neatly and quickly. They are also handy for cutting up cooked carrots, cooked potatoes, butter, margarine, bananas, and other soft foods.

PASTRY BRUSHES can be used for a wide variety of jobs, such as applying butter to toast, French toast, or pancakes and for oiling frying pans, steam table pans, and baking sheets. Care must be taken to be sure they are carefully sanitized after each use and discarded before bristles start to break off or fall out.

LEARNING ACTIVITY

GET READY: Prepare five quarts of soup (or liquid to represent soup). Get 10 soup bowls, a 2 oz ladle and a 6 oz ladle.

DO: Ladles are marked according to the number of ounces they will hold. Ask someone to help by timing you while you serve the soup.

Method I: Use a 2 oz ladle to serve 5 bowls of soup (about 6 oz per serving).

How many minutes were required?_____minutes

Method II: Use a 6 oz ladle, the exact size of the desired portion, to serve 5 bowls of soup.

How many minutes were required?_____minutes

EVALUATE: Which method required the least time?_____

Was either method neater (less spills on the rim) than the other?_____

If so, which method was better?_____

What was the difference in time required for the two method?_____minutes

Divide by 5 for time per bowl._____minutes

How many times is soup served in your facility each week?_____

How many portions are served each time?_____

Multiply the number of times soup is served each week times the number of portions served each time. Multiply this (the number of portions per week) times the minutes saved per bowl to determine the time saved by using the more efficient method.

What was the time saved each week?_____

SUMMARY: Work is done more efficiently and time is saved by using the best available equipment for the job.

PRINCIPLE 7 . . .

Locate Activity in Normal Work Areas When Possible

To improve productivity and to work as efficiently as possible it is important to define the ideal work areas on both the horizontal and vertical planes. Whenever possible arrange your work to be within these areas to save energy.

NORMAL HORIZONTAL WORK AREA

The space on the work surface within which work is done with the least energy is called the normal horizontal work area. [83] To find your normal horizontal work area, make an arc over the work surface by holding the upper arm comfortably close to the side and swinging from the elbow (Fig. 40).

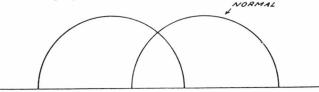

Fig. 40. Normal work area — horizontal plane

Work done in the normal work area uses the hand and forearm but does not require the use of the upper arm or body. Since most work involves the use of both hands, the total normal work area includes that space covered by the combined arcs of the two forearms.

63

MAXIMUM HORIZONTAL WORK AREA

The space on the work surface within which work is done with an average amount of energy is called the maximum horizontal work area. To find your maximum horizontal work area, make an arc over the work surface by extending the full arm outward and swinging from the shoulder (Fig. 41).

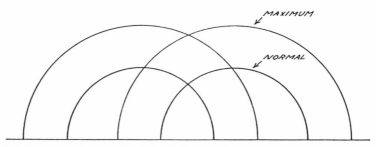

Fig. 41. Maximum work area — horizontal plane

Work that is done in the maximum work area uses the whole arm but does not require the use of the shoulders or other parts of the body. The total maximum work area includes the space covered by the combined arcs of the two extended arms.

Work done in the normal work area requires less energy than work done in the maximum work area. To test this principle, mark two imaginary spots on the work table: one 18 inches from the edge of the table and the other 2 inches from the edge of the table. Scrub these imaginary spots using eight strokes for each. Which spot required the least energy and muscle pull?

[84]   Work that is done outside the normal and maximum work areas causes body strain. It is extremely tiring to work outside the maximum work area when it is done repeatedly or when heavy articles are lifted. To test this principle, place two No. 5 bags of salt, sugar, or flour on the work table: one located at the edge of the table and the other 30 inches away from the edge of the table. Lift the two bags in turn, using both hands to support the weight. Which bag required the most energy and muscle strain?

MAKING SANDWICHES

When making sandwiches, arrange the ingredients as close as possible to the normal work area. The first ingredient needed is bread. Day-old sandwich bread is firm enough for easy spreading, yet not too dry. The second ingredient needed is butter or margarine. Soften butter or margarine at room temperature and then cream it until it has food-spreading consistency. When the filling to be used is soft, such as peanut butter, save the extra step of buttering the bread. Beat the butter and peanut butter in the mixer to make a single spread. The third ingredient needed is the filling. Filling that is soft may be prepared in an electric mixer. This takes less time and effort and assures an easy-to-spread consistency. Prepare the filling just before using. Foods such as tomatoes, cheese, and meats should be evenly sliced in advance of use and stored in the refrigerator. Cross-stack sliced ingredients such as cheese and meat so they can be quickly and easily picked up and used in sandwich preparation. The fourth ingredient needed is lettuce. Wash it thoroughly and separate the leaves carefully so they can be easily grasped. Allow lettuce to drain and crisp in the refrigerator until needed.

Collect the items of equipment and tools that will be used in sandwich making and arrange them in the normal work area. The first tools that will be needed are scoops. They provide a means of easy, accurate portioning of the filling mixture and are available in a wide range of sizes and capacities. Select the size of scoop that will provide the amount of filling to be served in the sandwiches. The size of the scoop indicates the number of scoops per quart.

Size	Measure
No. 8	½ c
No. 12	⅓ c
No. 16	¼ c
No. 20	3⅕ T
No. 24	2⅔ T
No. 30	2⅕ T

The second piece of equipment needed is a cutting board.

The cutting board or counter top should be nonporous and spotlessly clean. Wooden cutting boards are difficult to sanitize, have a tendency to splinter, and are unacceptable in many states.

The third piece of equipment needed is a spatula. A long spatula with a blade 1½ inches wide and long enough to reach across a slice of bread should be used for spreading. This makes it easy to spread the butter and filling in a single easy stroke without lifting the bread with the other hand.

The next items needed are knives. Two knives should be available: a paring knife for removing spots and paring, and a long knife for slicing. Both must be kept sharp.

Other supplies and equipment are needed. Waxed paper, plastic wrap, damp towels, plastic bags, and pans should be on hand for quick, correct storage.

NORMAL VERTICAL WORK AREA

[*85*]   Each hand has its normal work space in the vertical plane as well as on the work surface. To find the normal vertical work space, make an arc by holding the upper arm comfortably close to the side and swinging the lower arm both up and down in a circle, bending it only at the elbow as shown by the smaller arc in Figure 42.

Work is less tiring if the work area is arranged so that it is not necessary for the elbow to be raised above shoulder level during the work process. An example of arranging work so the elbows are not raised above shoulder level could be the filling and stacking of muffin pans. Place the bowl of batter on a lower cart or stool so that the

Fig. 42. Work areas — vertical plane

rim of the bowl is level with the muffin pan on the counter. Use a scoop to portion the batter. To avoid any long reach, fill the half of the pan closest to the bowl of batter, then turn the muffin pan and finish filling it. Several pans may be filled and stacked before transferring them to the oven.

The normal vertical work area indicates the space that should be used for storage of frequently used and heavy items. Store frequently used items where they are easily accessible. This is the area in which work is done with the least effort.

MAXIMUM VERTICAL WORK AREA

The maximum vertical work area is determined by using the extended arm. Make an arc with an easy upward and downward reach from the shoulder shown by the larger arc in Figure 42. Store less frequently used items in less desirable storage space. The maximum vertical work area indicates the space that should be used to store less frequently used and lightweight items. Straining to reach articles outside this area is tiring, particularly if the article to be lifted is heavy or reaching is done repeatedly.

Heavy and bulky containers are usually stored near the floor. This makes it necessary to do countless jobs of lifting and [86] carrying each day. Lifting should be done by holding the trunk erect while bending the knees to reach the level of the article to be lifted. This allows the leg and thigh muscles to carry the weight. Bending forward at the hip and keeping the legs straight throws the strain on the back muscles and may cause injury. The heavier the object to be lifted, the more important it is for you to maintain correct body position since you have the extra weight to lift in addition to your own body weight. Hold the weight close to your body. When an object to be lifted is out of the maximum work area in the vertical plane, it is particularly important that the object be well within that area horizontally. The reverse is equally true.

LEARNING ACTIVITY

GET READY: Prepare a product like cake or bar cookies in two bun pans. Cut them into portions according to the recipe. Get eight large trays or bun pans, a stack of small plates and two spatulas each 2 inches wide.

DO: **Method I:** Transfer the cut portions from the baking pan to plates without repositioning either the pan of product or the pan or tray on which the plates are placed. Have a helper time you as you work if you are not able to easily see a clock.

How long did it take to transfer all the portions from the pan to the plates?_____minutes

Method II: Position the baking pan and trays of plates on a cart or counter that is approximately 24 inches wide. Work with a partner to transfer the cut portions from the baking pan to the plates. Each worker will start from the closest edge and work toward the centers of both the pan of product and the trays of plates.

How long did it take to transfer all the portions from the pan to the plates?_____minutes

EVALUATE: How many minutes longer did the first method take than the second method? Note: Remember to divide the second method time by two because it was done by two people. _____minutes

How many pans of food do you portion each week?_____pans

How much time would be saved using the method using the shorter reaches? Multiply the number of pans times the minutes saved per pan. _____minutes

How much time would be saved each month (minutes per week times 4.3)?_____minutes

How much time would be saved each year (minutes per week times 52 or minutes per month times 12)?_____minutes

Multiply this by the hourly wage of the person doing the work.

_____dollars saved using the efficient method.

SUMMARY: Work is done more quickly and efficiently when it is in the normal work area and long reaches are avoided.

PRINCIPLE 8 . . .

Store Materials in an Orderly Manner

Storage is an operation that occurs in every foodservice department regardless of size or type of service. Poor storage results in hidden costs that affect operating efficiency.

STORAGE ARRANGEMENT

Frequently used items are stored in normal work areas, and less frequently used items are stored in the maximum work area. Rarely used items are stored outside the two areas, perhaps in a storeroom or storage closet.

[88]   In a storage drawer frequently used tools should be arranged in an orderly manner and as near as possible to the front of the top one or two drawers. Seldom used items may be stored in the lower drawers.

[89]   Store small equipment and needed supplies as close as possible to the place where they will be used. If storage space is not adequate in an area, it may be helpful to add some space through the use of a mobile cart.

Be sure there are enough drawers and racks in convenient locations so that the necessary knives, spoons, whips, etc., are stored at the places they will be used. It is a relatively simple process to add a drawer under a work table if there is not

71

enough existing drawer space. Keep the tools in the drawers and racks in an orderly arrangement so they can be quickly seen and easily removed.

Store each item at the point of its first use. Employees should not have to walk back and forth to obtain utensils and materials they need. When the point-of-first-use storage concept is applied, storage areas are spread in a logical pattern. A few possible placements include: potatoes and other tuberous vegetables near the peeler; knives and cutting boards near the table where they are used; mixer bowls, beaters, and paddles near the mixer; containers to be filled with water near the sink or water supply; pans to be filled with mashed potatoes by the mixer; pans to be filled with frozen vegetables to be cooked in the work area near the steamer; paper and plastic cooking utensils near the microwave oven; napkins and flatware near the serving area; cake pans to be filled with batter near the mixer; pie pans near the pie-rolling machine; beverages near the serving area.

PREPARING COFFEE

One task performed daily in foodservice facilities is that of preparing coffee (Fig. 43). To see whether that area of your kitchen is as conveniently arranged as it might be, do this simple exercise:

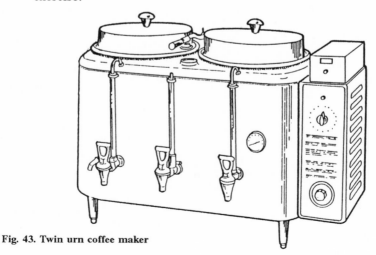

Fig. 43. Twin urn coffee maker

STEP ONE. The first step is to draw a rough sketch of the
kitchen. Include the main pieces of equipment and the
storage areas that are involved in coffeemaking.

STEP TWO. The second step is to record each process. To do
this, show the present procedure by using a blue or black
pen. Make an X at the starting point. Draw a line to follow the
path used to proceed through the job. For example, the path
might go from the starting point to a storage rack for a gallon
measure, to the sink for water, to the urn where the brewing
takes place, to the drawer where the filters are kept, to the urn
where the filter will be installed, to the storeroom for the coffee,
to the urn where the coffee will be measured into the filter, to
the cupboard were the cups are stored, to the urn where a
sample will be checked for quality.

STEP THREE. The third step is to question each detail. For
example, can supplies or equipment be rearranged to make
the work more efficient? Can any step of the procedure be
eliminated without adversely affecting the quality of the product?
Can any two steps be combined so that less effort is required to
perform the job?

STEP FOUR. The fourth step is to work out a better method.
Think of ways that time and steps could be reduced in the
process of brewing coffee. For example, an overhead faucet may
be installed above the urn so that it is not necessary to carry
water. Coffee may be stored in the stand under the coffee urn so
that the supply is always conveniently at hand. The filters may be
stored in a drawer in the urn stand. Coffee may be purchased
premeasured so no measuring is required. Coffee may be purchased encased in the filter so separate supplies of filters and
coffee are not needed. Cups and saucers may be stored in a
mobile cart, which can be rolled to a position next to the coffee
urn until needed.

STEP FIVE. The fifth step is to apply the new method. When all
possible improvements have been made, try the new method
several times until it becomes familiar. Write down the new
method so it will be available as a handy reference or as a guide

in teaching the routine to new employees.

To evaluate any study, compare the improved method with the original one. With a red pen, draw the lines on your sketch to follow the path used to proceed through the job using the new method.

This same exercise can be used to compare an old method and an improved method for any task you may select, for example, cleaning the coffee urn, making cooked cereal, portioning cake squares, or pouring orange juice.

STORAGE SPACE

Assign a definite, fixed space for each piece of equipment. When everything has a place, it becomes everyone's job to see that each item is returned to its assigned spot so that it will be ready for the next use without wasting time in searching. A good motto is: A Place for Everything and Everything in Its Place. This should be done before storage space is built, but in many areas better planning and use can be made of the storage space already provided.

[90] Waste space is often found between shelves. It is recommended that storeroom shelves for canned food be adjusted to fit the size container being stored on it. Adjustable shelving is recommended because of its greater flexibility. Allow 2 inches above the container to have room for hands to re-

Fig. 44. Adjustable shelves

move the product from the shelves without abrasions. Shelves 12 inches apart are fine for gallon jars, those 9 inches apart will accommodate No. 10 and No. 5 cans. Provide shallow shelves for baby food and flat boxes. Shelves that are 21 inches wide allow three No. 10 cans, four No. 5 cans, and six No. 2 or No. 2½ cans to be lined up (Fig. 44). If the shelving is arranged to allow traffic on both sides, it may be wise to get shelves that are 42 inches deep and will accommodate twice as many cans.

STORAGE CONTAINERS

Storage space will be more efficiently used if the food is trimmed and put in standard-sized containers than if it is stored untrimmed in boxes of assorted shapes and sizes. For example, when receiving lettuce, celery, or other bulky vegetables that require washing and trimming before use, clean and trim them at once. Then store them in standard-sized baskets or pans that can be taken directly to the point of use.

[91] Store like items in front of each other. This enables workers to quickly locate needed supplies. If like items are placed together in an orderly manner, the amount on hand can be determined at a glance.

[92] Label drawers and shelves to save time and ensure the proper placement of incoming supplies. This practice can also save time when taking a physical inventory.

The wise placement and use of pans may mean a savings of both time and labor. Multipurpose pans can be placed in freezers, refrigerators, ranges, ovens, and serving tables. This eliminates the frequent transfers required between storage, cooking, and service and reduces the number of pans to be washed.

The use of standard steam table pans instead of special baking pans for meat loaf and similar foods will reduce the number of pans to be purchased and stored, the time necessary for handling and transferring the product from baking pans to serving pans, and the number of pans to be washed and put away. It is important that pans receiving much use at such a wide range of temperatures be of heavy-duty stainless steel (18 gauge).

Stainless steel steam table pans are easy to clean, stack, and handle. They are constructed with smooth corners and have no sharp edges. Pans not requiring as much durability and such a wide temperature range may be made of a high quality polycarbonate that will go from $-50°$ F to $212°$ F or of polysulfon that will go from $-40°$ F to $300°$ F, making it usable in microwave ovens.

A few large (18 × 26 inch) baking pans instead of many small pans should be used in the preparation of items such as cake. This will reduce the time spent in measuring batter into pans, the handling of pans in and out of the oven, and the number of pans to be washed and put away.

[*93*] Basic steam table pans are now available in many sizes and with depths of 2¼, 4, and 6 inches (Fig. 45).

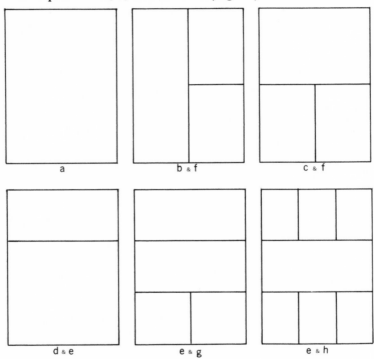

Fig. 45. Steam table pan size combinations

a. full — 12 × 20 inches   e. one-third — 6 × 12 inches
b. half-long — 6 × 20 inches   f. one-fourth — 6 × 10 inches
c. half-standard — 10 × 12 inches   g. one-sixth — 6 × 6 inches
d. two-thirds — 12 × 13 inches   h. one-ninth — 4 × 6 inches

A combination of small steam table pans (Fig. 45) may be used in the serving table. This makes it possible to have part of each menu item on the serving table when serving begins.

LEARNING ACTIVITY

GET READY: Get a tape measure or measuring stick at least 4 feet long.

DO: Check the amount and condition of the shelf space in your facility. See what containers are being stored, how large they are, and how far apart the shelves are to allow for their storage.

Container	Height of Can	Shelf Height
a_____	_____	_____
b_____	_____	_____
c_____	_____	_____
d_____	_____	_____
e_____	_____	_____

EVALUATE: Is there any wasted space?_____

Are there places that space could be saved if all items on the shelf were the same height and the shelf above it were lowered to a position 1½ inches above the can or box?_____

How many inches were saved?_____inches

How long was that shelf?_____feet

Was the space saved enough to allow you to add another shelf on the top?_____

Is it easier to work with shelves that are organized and orderly?_____

SUMMARY: Space can be saved and efficiency increased when materials are stored in an orderly manner.

Evaluating Methods and Costs

If you are able to develop a new method of doing a particular task, it is then necessary to judge its value according to these three criteria: energy, quality, and time.

ENERGY

To determine whether there was a savings of energy, ask such questions as: Is the worker less tired when using the new method than when the other method was used? Is the worker less reluctant to do the job when using the new method than when the other method was used?

QUALITY

To determine whether there was an improvement in quality, ask such questions as: Is the product as good or better in appearance, flavor, and quality than it was when the other method was used? Are the portions more uniform when using the new method than when using the other method?

TIME

To determine whether there was a savings of time, ask such questions as: Is less time spent in accomplishing the same amount of work? Is less time required to set up the work area? Is less time required to clean up the work area?

To determine the amount of time saved in performing a task, first select the product to be tested, for example, cookies. Prepare 50 portions of the product by the old method and record the time spent. For example, 10 minutes. Then prepare 50 portions of the same product using the new method and record the time spent. For example, 4 minutes. In this case, the savings in time were 6 minutes for every 50-portion amount that was prepared. Assume that 300 cookies are baked each week in the facility. Divide the number of cookies baked each week (300) by the number of cookies in each batch (50) to determine the batches used each week. Multiply the batches baked each week (6) by the number of weeks in a year (52) to determine the batches used each year. That shows 312 batches are used each year. Multiply the batches baked each year (312) by the minutes saved for each batch (6) to determine the minutes saved each year. Each year 1,872 minutes were saved. Divide the minutes saved in baking cookies each year (1,872) by the minutes in an hour (60) to convert the minutes saved into hours and minutes. Each year 31 hours and 12 minutes were saved in just the cookie-making process.

FOOD COST

Another method of placing a value on the food produced and the work done is knowing the cost. This may be accomplished in a number of ways. Administrators and accountants may prefer one method of figuring cost over another.

GROSS FOOD COST. Gross food cost is found by totaling the cost of each ingredient used in preparing the day's menu.

GROSS LABOR COST. Gross labor cost is found by totaling the cost (hours spent in food service x hourly wage) of each employee who was involved the foodservice operation; be sure to include all employee time contributed. This includes such things as purchasing; menu writing; record keeping; food distribution; dishwashing; and floor, wall, and window cleaning that may be done by other departments.

TOTAL GROSS COST. Total gross cost is found by adding together gross food cost and gross labor cost.

FOOD COST PER PATIENT-DAY. Food cost per patient-day, which is done in many health care facilities, is found by dividing gross food cost by total patient count.

FOOD COST PER MEAL. Food cost per meal, which is done in school foodservice, college feeding, correctional facilities, and some health care facilities, is found by dividing gross food cost by total meals served. Be sure to include all meals produced. This may include those for student nurses, patients' guests, board dinners, free meals to particular employees, and nourishments. You may choose to count nourishments as ⅓, ¼, or ⅕ of a meal, or you may not count them at all. Whatever policy you choose, be sure to have it recorded and follow the same plan consistently.

LABOR COST PER MEAL. Labor cost per meal is found by dividing gross labor cost by total meals served.

LABOR COST PER DAY. Labor cost per day is found by dividing gross labor cost by patient-days or patient count.

PORTION COST. Portion cost is found by totaling the cost of all ingredients used in the recipe and dividing by the number of portions it yields. This is the most accurate method of obtaining food cost but also the most time-consuming. To save time and labor when correcting portion cost as prices change, make corrections to only the ingredients for which a change in cost has occurred. This could be done on the same form to reduce paperwork (see Fig. 46).

PORTION COST

Recipe item_____

Number of servings_____

Cost per serving_____ Date_____

Ingredient	Amount	Unit price	Cost
Total			

Note: Multiply the amount of each ingredient times the unit price to determine the cost of each ingredient. Total these amounts to find the cost of the recipe. Divide this total cost by the number of servings to find the cost per serving.

Fig. 46. Portion cost calculation sheet. (Reprinted from Lynne Nannen Ross, *Purchasing for Food Service* © 1985 by Iowa State University Press.)

MINUTES PER MEAL. Minutes per meal are found by dividing total meals served by the total minutes spent by employees contributing to foodservices. If the number of staff employees is exactly the same every day, this may be calculated for one day. If the number of employees varies depending on the day of the week, it may be more accurate to calculate for an entire week, thus averaging to compensate for the fluctuations.

If the production costs as described above are known, the use of preprocessed foods can be intelligently evaluated to determine whether or not money can be saved through their use. Preprocessed items such as peeled potatoes, prebaked potatoes, sectioned grapefruit and oranges, premixed rolls and cakes, instant puddings, precooked or partially cooked frozen products, frozen fruits and vegetables, sliced and grated cheeses, heat-and-eat products, and brown-and-serve products may be evaluated as to savings when compared with the same product made in the facility.

COST COMPARISON

PREPREPARED CAKE. Select a product to be tested, such as white cake. Record the cost of a single portion of preprepared cake (21 cents). Record the cost of a single portion of cake prepared in the facility (11 cents). Subtract the cost of a portion of cake prepared in the facility (11 cents) from the cost of a portion of preprepared cake (21 cents) to determine the difference in food cost. The difference is 10 cents per serving. Based on just this information the cake made in the facility would be a better buy.

Record the labor time required portioning and serving a portion of preprepared cake (1 min.). Multiply the time used in serving a portion of preprepared cake (1 min.) by the average wage per hour ($7.20) to find the labor cost. (Note: Divide labor cost per hour by 60 to find cost per minute.) The labor cost of serving a portion of preprepared cake is 12 cents. Remember when calculating labor cost, to get a true picture of the real cost we must include not only the pay per hour of the employee, but all the benefits they receive such as insurance, vacation, and investments subsidized by administration. Record the labor time required in preparing and serving a portion of cake made in the facility (4 min.). This may be less if large amounts are prepared or more if very small amounts are made.

FACILITY-MADE CAKE. Multiply the time used in preparing and serving a portion of cake made in the facility (4 min.) by the average wage per hour ($8.40) to find the cost. This will combine the time and average wage of the baker with the time and average wage of the server. (Note: Divide cost per hour by 60 to find cost per minute.) The labor cost of preparing and serving a portion of cake made in the facility is 48 cents.

The difference in labor time is determined by subtracting the time used in serving a portion of preprepared cake (1 min.) from the time used in preparing and serving a portion of cake made in the facility (4 min.). The difference is 3 minutes.

The difference in labor cost is found by subtracting the labor cost of serving a portion of preprepared cake (12 cents) from the labor cost of preparing and serving a portion of cake made in the facility (48 cents). The difference in labor cost is 36 cents. The total cost of a portion of preprepared cake is found by adding the food cost (21 cents) and the labor cost (12 cents) for a total cost of 33 cents.

The total cost of a portion of cake prepared and served in the facility is found by adding the food cost (11 cents) and the labor cost (48 cents) for a total cost of 59 cents.

MAKING A DECISION. By subtracting the cost of one from the other we can determine the difference in cost is 26 cents per portion. In this example, the preprepared cake was lower in cost. This may not always be true, so it will be necessary to compute the cost as we have just done to know the facts that are required to make a wise judgment. When making this kind of comparison it may be easier to use the cost and time for a whole cake rather than a portion. Be sure cakes of equal size are being compared. The food cost, labor cost, and total cost for the whole cake would then be divided by the number of portions to determine the cost per portion. Other factors that may affect your decision-making process with regard to the choice between making or buying a particular product are the availability of an individual who can prepare a product of equal quality with that of the purchased one; the availability of a person with time to spend preparing the product; the quality of the product; the nutritional value of the product; and the acceptability of the product by the consumer.

Make Your Program Work

Apply the eight PRINCIPLES OF WORK SIMPLIFICA-
TION to develop better methods of solving the problems in a
foodservice facility.

In the search for possible solutions to foodservice problems,
the following four approaches should be considered.

1. ELIMINATE the unnecessary work
2. COMBINE operations
3. REARRANGE the sequence of operations
4. SIMPLIFY the necessary operations

ELIMINATE UNNECESSARY WORK

Far too much work done today is not necessary. In many
instances parts of the task or the process should not be a subject
for simplification or improvement but may be eliminated. The
[94] task thought to be one of the lengthiest and most repetitious in
foodservice departments is dishwashing. At this point we should
ask ourselves why the operation is necessary. Can the entire task
of washing tableware be eliminated by using all disposable items?
If so, the task is completely eliminated, making simplification
unnecessary. However, if, as in many facilities, disposables do not
meet the standards of foodservice desired, consider some of the
other possibilities. For example, can part of the task be eliminated by using some disposables, such as hot and cold cups, for
nourishments in health care facilities? Another way in which part
of the task of dishwashing can be eliminated is by using prepack-
[95] aged portion-control items instead of serving individual portions
in containers that need to be washed. Products that can be
purchased and served in disposables are milk, cream, salad

87

dressing, catsup, mustard, tartar sauce, sugar and sugar substitutes, syrup, jelly, honey, sherbet and ice cream, and pudding.

COMBINE OPERATIONS

It is possible to make work easier by combining two or more operations or by making some changes in method that permit operations to be combined. For example, when it has been decided that the tableware being washed is necessary in the operation, effort should be concentrated on combining the [96] required steps in an efficient sequence. Combine the operation of sorting and presoaking of silverware by sorting it directly into plastic cylinders. Then place the cylinders in a basket and lower them into the soak sink. After the cylinders of silverware have been soaked, place them in a dish rack and wash them in the dishwashing machine. This procedure combines the drying and sorting operations that would normally occur on the clean end of the dishwashing machine. When the silverware in the cylinders has been washed, each cylinder is inverted into a clean, empty one. It is then ready for use in the cafeteria line or for tray service.

Avoid handling dishes more than once by loading them directly into dish racks as they are scraped. This will combine the steps of tray breakdown, plate scraping, and rack loading. To do this efficiently, work with both hands at the same time. Place the dish racks so that the hand that picks up an item from the tray will deliver it to the rack. Crossing of the arms and transferring items from one hand to the other is tiring and time-consuming.

REARRANGE SEQUENCE

It is desirable to question the order in which the operations are performed when attempting to improve efficiency. The trays should keep moving from the cart or conveyer on which they are brought to the dishwashing area. They should keep moving forward through the operations of (1) removing paper, (2) removing plate waste, (3) soaking silverware, (4) racking glassware, (5) stacking or racking china, and (6) racking trays. If the direction of travel is ever away from the dishwashing machine, it would be advisable to check the reason. It may be because one of the following is located incorrectly: (1) the paper-waste container, (2) the food-waste container, (3) the garbage disposer, (4) the overhead shelf, or (5) the sprayer. In some cases a backward direction of travel can be corrected with little difficulty. For example, it may be possible to move the paper-waste container to a more convenient location. Many times the assistance of the engineering department and possibly the approval of the administrator will be required, particularly if a major change such as relocating a garbage disposer is involved. If you feel strongly that relocation of some of the equipment could improve the situation, it would be wise to discuss it with your superiors.

SIMPLIFY

After the process has been studied and all major improvements that seem worthwhile have been made, the next step is to analyze each operation in the process to try to simplify all motions. In other words, the overall picture is studied first and major changes are made, then the small details of the work are studied. Question each hand and arm motion. It is very difficult to see problems when they occur in your own work. A better way is to observe fellow workers as they do their jobs. This is particularly true if the observation can be made at a time when the worker is not aware of being watched. Often we will find that by watching other people work and seeing their inefficiencies we become aware of ways in which our own work may be improved.

A work simplification program can be used to make any job easier if you will follow these four steps:

[97] OBSERVE — Have an open mind and maintain a questioning attitude.
Who should do it?
What is to be done?
Where should it be done?
Why is it really necessary?
When should it be done?

How should it be done?

[*98*] **THINK**— Study the facts, not opinions.
Find the causes, not effects.
Work with reasons, not excuses.
Consider others' ideas, not just your own.

[*99*] **DECIDE**— Use all the facts, reasons, causes, and ideas in making the decisions.

[*100*] **ACT**— Check with your supervisor, then put the plan into effect.